BIG
BEASTS
Camel

Stephanie Turnbull

Published by Smart Apple Media,
an imprint of Black Rabbit Books
P.O. Box 3263, Mankato, Minnesota, 56002
www.blackrabbitbooks.com

Designed by Hel James
Edited by Mary-Jane Wilkins

Library of Congress Cataloging-in-Publication Data
Turnbull, Stephanie.
  Camel / Stephanie Turnbull.
    pages cm. -- (Big beasts)
  Summary: "Describes the characteristics of Camels
and their life and habitat"-- Provided by publisher.
  Audience: K to Grade 3.
  Includes index.
  ISBN 978-1-62588-164-9
  1. Camels--Juvenile literature. I. Title.
  QL737.U54T87 2015
  599.63'62--dc23
                          2014003966

Photo acknowledgements
l = left, r = right, t = top, b = bottom
title page Roman Gorielov/Shutterstock; page 3 Ivan
Pavlov/Shutterstock; 4, 5 iStockphoto/Thinkstock; 6 Maxim
Petrichuk, 7 Banana Republic images/both Shutterstock;
8 alersandr hunta, 9 Polina Truver/both Shutterstock;
10 Rambleon/Shutterstock; 11 iStockphoto/Thinkstock;
12, 13 iStockphoto/Thinkstock; 14 Maxim Petrichuk,
15 John Carnemolla/both Shutterstock; 16 Berit Kessler,
17 Andrea Willmore/both Shutterstock; 18 OlegD/
Shutterstock; 19 iStockphoto/Thinkstock; 20, 21 iStockphoto/
Thinkstock; 22l iStockphoto/Thinkstock, r Sergej
Razvodovskij/Shutterstock; 23 iStockphoto/Thinkstock
Cover tezzstock/Shutterstock

Printed in China

DAD0059
032014
9 8 7 6 5 4 3 2 1

Contents

Camels are

huge!

Desert Giants

Camels are tough, strong mammals with hooves.

Desert tribes use camels to carry heavy loads over huge distances.

All camels have fatty humps on their backs.

Tall and Leggy

Most camels are called dromedaries.
They live in hot, dry lands in the
Middle East, Africa, and South Asia.

Dromedaries have one tall hump. Long, thin legs keep their bodies high above the scorching sand.

Slow and Shaggy

A few camels live in the rocky hills
and stony deserts of Central Asia.

These shorter, bulkier camels are called Bactrians.
Bactrians have two humps.

Thick, wooly coats protect them from
biting winds and freezing temperatures.

Bumpy Bodies

Camels survive in deserts because their bodies don't lose much water.

A big drink can last them for days.

They don't sweat and
their pee is a thick syrup
with hardly any water in it!

Camels use the fat in their
humps to create extra water.
As they use up this fat store,
their humps shrink and slump.

Desert Sand

Camels keep *swirling* desert sand out of their eyes with two rows of long eyelashes.

Thick hair stops sand blowing in their ears —and they can even close their nostrils.

Extra **w i d e** hooves let them walk over sand without sinking.

Finding Food

Camel owners let camels
find their own food.

Camels roam in herds, searching
for plants. They aren't fussy!

They grasp twigs in thick, rubbery lips. Their mouths are so tough that thorns don't hurt them.

Camels swallow their food then burp it up later to chew.

15

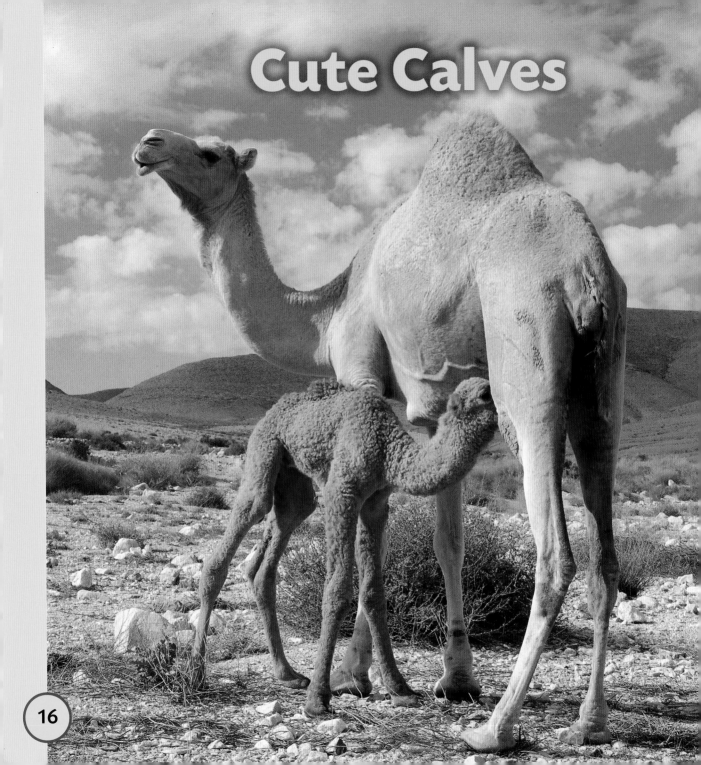

Cute Calves

Female camels give birth to one baby at a time.

Babies are called calves. They can run only a few hours after they are born.

Calves drink their mother's milk and stay close to her for two years.

Hard Workers

Camels are calm, patient animals.
They are easily trained to wear saddles
on their humps and carry goods or people.

They kneel to be loaded or to rest.

They are often decorated with **colorful** tassels and bright beads for festivals.

Living Wild

Some camels
don't have owners.

Large herds of dromedaries roam free
in Central Australia. They often eat
farmers' crops and damage fences.

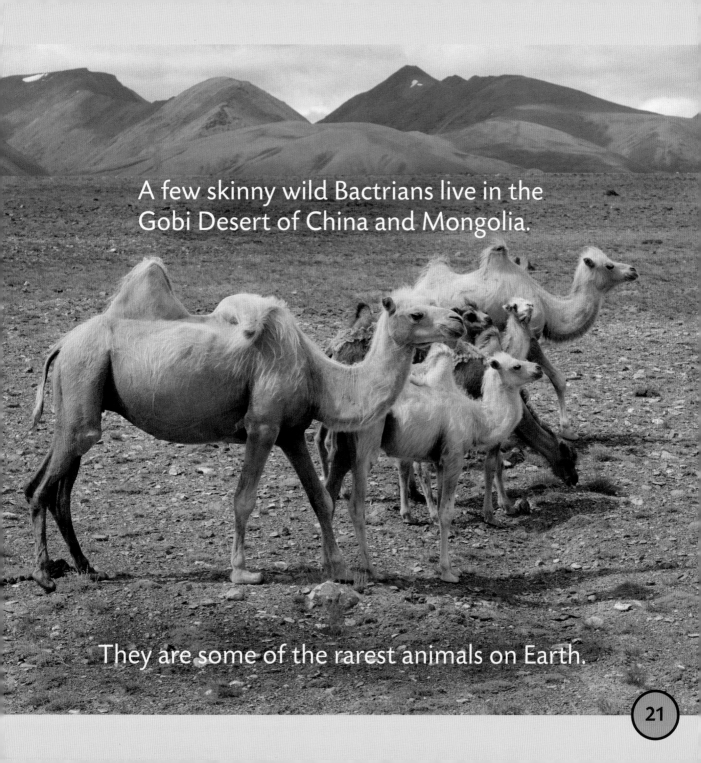

A few skinny wild Bactrians live in the Gobi Desert of China and Mongolia.

They are some of the rarest animals on Earth.

BIG Facts

A big camel could carry the weight of you and ten friends.

Camels have 34 large, sharp teeth for chewing tough plants.

Camels can gulp down about seven big bucketfuls of water in ten minutes!

Camels use their long, curved necks to reach high branches and to drink without bending their legs.

Useful Words

herd
A group of animals that live together.

hoof
The hard covering on the front of a camel's foot.

tribe
A group of people. Many desert tribes are farmers or travelers.

Index

Web Link

Visit this web site for cool camel facts:
www.kidskonnect.com/subjectindex/13-categories/animals/19-camels.html